Th Try to Laugh Challenge

Joke Book

Valentine's Day Edition

Hundreds of Jokes

That Kids and Family Will Enjoy

With Fun Illustrations

Riddleland

Check out some of the fun illustrations that come with the jokes

More fun illustrations

Table of Contents

Introduction

"Life is filled with lots of things that make it all worthwhile, but none is better than your little smile."

We would like to personally thank you for purchasing this book. **The Try Not to Laugh Challenge Joke Book: Valentine's Day Edition** is different from other joke books. It is not meant to be read alone, but instead, it is a game to be played with siblings, friends, family or between two people that would like to prove who is a better comedian. Time to see who has the funny bone in the family!

These jokes are written to be fun and easy to read. Children learn best when they are playing. Reading can help increase vocabulary and comprehension. They have also many other benefits such as:

- **Bonding** – It is an excellent way for parents and their children to spend some quality time and create some fun and memorable memories.

- **Confidence Building** - When parents give the riddles, it creates a safe environment for children to blurt out answers even if they are incorrect. This helps the children to develop self-confidence in expressing themselves.

- **Improve Vocabulary** – Jokes are usually written in easy to advanced words, therefore children will need to understand these words before they can share the jokes.

- **Better reading comprehension** – Many children can read at a young age but may not understand the context of the sentences. Riddles can help develop children's interest to comprehend the context before they can share it with their friends.

- **Sense of humor** -Funny creative jokes can help children develop their sense of humor while getting their brains working.

Rules of the Game!

The goal is to make your opponent laugh

- Face your opponent
- Stare at them!
- Make funny faces and noises to throw your opponent off
- Take turns reading the jokes out loud to each other
- When someone laughs, the other person wins a point

The first-person to get 5 points, is crowned The Joke Master!

Alert: Try Not to Laugh Challenge Bonus Jokes

Join our special Facebook Group at
Riddleland For Kids

or

send an email to:

Riddleland@riddlelandforkids.com

and you will get the following

- 50 Bonus Jokes and Riddles
- An Entry in Our Monthly Giveaway of $50 Amazon Gift card!
- Early Access to new books

We draw a new winner each month and will contact you via email or the facebook group.
Good Luck!

Chapter 1: The Hugs and Kisses Challenge

"If you have only one smile in you, give it to the people you love." ~ Maya Angelou

What did one raspberry say to the other on Valentine's Day?

I love you berry much!

What did the stamp say to the Valentine's Day card?

I'm stuck on you!

Why do skunks love Valentine's Day?

They are very scent-imental creatures.

What did the cucumber say to the pickle?

You mean a great dill to me.

What did the farmer give his wife for Valentine's Day?

Hogs and kisses.

What did one watermelon say to the other watermelon on Valentine's Day?

You are one in a melon!

What did the lightbulb say to his girlfriend?

I love you a whole watt!

What did one volcano say to the other volcano?

I lava you!

What did the baker say to his Valentine's Day sweetheart?

I'm dough-nuts about you!

What do you call a ghost's true love?

His ghoul-friend.

Why is Valentine's Day a good day for a party?

Because you can really party hearty!

What did the painter say to her sweetheart?

I love you with all of my art.

What did Robin Hood say to his girlfriend?

Sherwood like to be your valentine.

Did you hear about the nearsighted porcupine?

He asked a pin cushion to be his valentine!

How can you tell that the calendar is popular?

It always has a date for Valentine's Day.

Why did the policewoman lock up her boyfriend?

He stole her heart.

Where do burgers take their Valentine's Day dates to dance?

To the meatball.

What did the girl sweet say to the boy sweet?

It's Valentine's Day and we're mint to be together.

What did the calculator tell the pencil on Valentine's Day?

You can count on me.

What did the cracker say to the marshmallow?

I love you s'more and s'more every single day!

Why did the scientist ask the laboratory to be their valentine?

Because they had such great chemistry together!

How did the mobile phone propose to his girlfriend?

He gave her a ring.

Why did the hotdog ask the bun to be its Valentine?

Because it really relished the time they had together!

Why was the taco so happy when the nachos asked it out for Valentine's Day?

It had bean hoping they'd ask all year!

What fruits enjoy hugs the most?

Avo-cuddles!

What did the ghost say to his Valentine's Day date?

You look so BOOtiful tonight.

Why did the banana go out with the prune?

Because it couldn't get a date.

Why didn't the flower get another date after that?

He was a garden variety!

What do you call two flowers that just started dating?

A budding romance!

What did the flower's Valentine's Day card read?

Aloe you vera much!

What did the flower say to his valentine?

I think you're dandy and I'm not lion!

What did one boat paddle say to the other?

Can I interest you in a little row-mance?

What do you say when you want a kiss from a flower?

Plant one on me!

What does toast call its valentine?

Its butter-half.

What happens when you fall in love with a pastry chef?

You get buttered up.

What flower gives the most kisses on Valentine's Day?

Tulips.

What did the flower say when it wanted a second

date?

I'll grow on you!

What do ghosts say to one another to show that

they care?

I love BOO!

How did the train pick his valentine?

He choo, choo, choose her.

What did the shy girl sweetcorn say to the boy sweetcorn on the evening before Valentine's Day?

Shucks, I'd like to ear from you on Valentine's Day.

Why did the boy put clothes on his Valentine's Day cards?

He heard that they had to be addressed.

What did the hamburger say to its valentine?

Time fries when I'm with you!

What did the rice say to its valentine?

I love you soy-sauce much!

What did the lemon say to the lime?

Lime yours if you'll have me!

What's the cutest vegetable in the garden?

Cute-cumbers!

What did the paper clip say to the magnet?

I find you very attractive.

What do you call a really small Valentine's Day card?

A valen-tiny.

Why couldn't the teddy bear finish all its Valentine's Day chocolates?

Because it was just too stuffed.

What did one nacho say to the other nacho?

This might be cheesy, but I think you're pretty grate!

Why did the lunch box ask the banana to be its Valentine?

Because it really had appeal.

What did the flower say after telling a joke?

I was pulling your leg!

Why do flowers drive so fast?

They put the petal to the metal!

What did the tree say to its valentine?

I wood never leaf you!

What did the cake say to woo its baker?

You bake me crazy!

Why should you marry a cherry?

They'll cherry-ish you forever!

What did the blueberry say to his girlfriend on Valentine's Day?

You blue me away and I love you berry, berry much.

What food is absolutely crazy about Valentine's Day chocolates?

A cocoa-nut

What did the chocolate syrup say to the ice cream?

I'm sweet on you!

Why did the M&M decide to go to college?

He wanted to be a Smarty.

Why did the doughnut visit the dentist?

She needed a chocolate filling.

What is an astronaut's favorite chocolate?

A Mars bar.

Why do whiteboards get so many Valentine's Day dates?

Because they're so remarkable!

What happens when prisoners fall in love?

They finish each other's sentences!

Why did the calligraphist get lots of valentines?

Everyone thought she had pretty I's!

Why don't diabetic vampires like Valentine's Day?

They can't have sweethearts!

What happened when the flower grew fed up with her Valentine's Day date?

She told him once and floral!

What kind of Valentine's Day sweet is never on time?

ChocoLATE.

Why did the flower take her Valentine's Day date back?

She rose above it!

How does a flower handle a bad Valentine's Day date?

It gets clover it!

What did the flower say to his wife when he brought her home a box of Valentine's Day chocolates?

I hope thistle cheer you up!

What did the pyramid say to its Valentine's Day date?

Are you a triangle? Because you're acute angle!

Why did the mushroom get a date for Valentine's Day?

Everyone thought he was a fungi (fun guy)!

What kind of flowers do you never give on Valentine's Day?

Cauliflower.

What did the coffee lover tell their Valentine's Day date?

Words cannot espresso how much you mean to me!

How did Frankenstein ask his crush out for Valentine's Day?

Would you be my Valenstein?

What happened when two lazy people went on a Valentine's Day date?

They didn't work out!

Why was the guy looking for a platonic valentine?

He was asking for a friend!

What happened to the travellers' relationship?

They grew distant!

Why does Miss Piggy have such good relationships?

She believes in Kermit-ment!

What's the difference between affection and adore?

You can't get your thumb caught in affection!

Why is it dangerous to give a Valentine's Day card to

someone that is lactose intolerant?

They're all too cheesy!

What did one mushroom say to the other mushroom

on Valentine's Day?

There's so mushroom in my heart for you!

What happened when the man fell in love with his

garden?

It made him wet his plants!

What happened when the two tennis players met?

It was lob at first sight!

What did the calculator say to its valentine?

Let me count the ways that I love you!

How did the deaf boy ask out his crush out for Valentine's Day?

"Will you be mime?"

What did the tomato's Valentine's Day card read?

I love you from my head tomato!

How does Han spend Valentine's Day?

Solo!

Why does your heart want to be your valentine?

It's always pumped for you!

Why did the girl ask the air conditioner to be her valentine?

He was a big fan of hers!

Why should you never break up with a soccer goalie?

Because they're a keeper!

What did the vegetable say to its valentine?

You make my heart-beet faster.

Why did the boy steal his valentine's glasses?

Because he heard love is blind!

What kind of wizard makes a pie for her Valentine?

A pie-romancer!

Where do tightrope performers meet their Valentine's Day dates?

On-line dating sites!

Why didn't the blood cell have a date for Valentine's Day?

He tried to get one but his efforts were in vein!

Did you hear the one about the flower that never bloomed?

It was a bud omen!

What do you call two flowers that are best friends?

Buds!

What did the Jedi say to her valentine?

Yoda one for me!

Why do campers make for such great valentines?

They're always intense!

What happened when the two vampires went out for Valentine's Day?

It was love at first bite!

Why shouldn't you ask a tennis player to be your valentine?

Because love means nothing to them!

What's the best chocolate to get your girlfriend for Valentine's Day?

Her-She kisses!

Why did the boy go to the doctor after Valentine's Day?

Because he heard that love was infectious!

What did the pizza tell the delivery box?

I love you with every pizza my heart!

Why did the barista ask out their valentine?

Because they were her cup of tea!

Why did the boy give his Valentine tacos instead of chocolate?

He was thinking outside the box!

What did the man with the broken leg tell his Valentine's Day date?

I've got a crutch on you!

Did Adam and Eve ever have a date?

No, but they had an apple.

Why did the boy put sweet under his pillow?

Because he wanted to have sweet dreams.

What did the flame say to all his friends when he found the perfect valentine?

I found the perfect match!

What did the drum say to the other drum on Valentine's Day?

My heart beats for you.

How did the vampire ask out his valentine?

He asked her out for a bite.

What did the fruit cocktail tell its valentine?

You're the pineapple of my eye!

What does a carpet salesman give his wife on Valentine's Day?

Rugs and kisses.

What did the baker say to his Valentine's Day date?

I only have pies for you!

What is the most attractive kind of fruit?

Fine-apple!

Why were the bears so madly in love?

Because they spent so much koala-ty time with each

other!

Why did the kid ask his maths teacher to be his

valentine?

Because she helped fix all his problems!

What did the pastry say to its Valentine's Day date?

I doughnut know what I would do without you!

Why didn't the skeleton want to send any Valentine's Day cards?
His heart wasn't in it.

What did the mermaid ask her valentine?

Whale, shell we go dancing?

What did the ice-cream cone say when the sun

asked it out for Valentine's Day?

I'm so happy, you always make me melt!

What did the pencil say to the paper?

I dot my I's on you!

Chapter 2: Sweet and Cute Animal Jokes

The Eskimos had fifty-two names for snow because it was important to them; there ought to be as many for love ~ Margaret Atwood

Why did the otter get married?

Because he met his significant otter!

What do you get when you kiss a dragon on Valentine's Day?

Third-degree burns on your lips.

What did the bee's sweetheart say back to him?

I love bee-ing with you, Honey!

What did the buck say to the doe on Valentine's Day?

You are very dear to me.

What did the boy sheep say to the girl sheep on Valentine's Day?

I love ewe!

What did the whale say to his sweetheart on Valentine's Day?

Whale you be mine?

What do you call two love birds on Valentine's Day?

Tweet hearts.

What is a monkey's favorite cookie?

Chocolate chimp

What did the squirrel give to his valentine?

Forget-me-nuts.

What did the girl sheep say back to the boy sheep?

You're not so baaaaaaa-d yourself!

Why did the chicken cross the road?

Because her valentine was on the other side.

Why did the mouse ask the keyboard to be her valentine?

It was her type!

What did the slug say to ask its crush to be its Valentine?

Will you be my valen-slime?

What did the dolphin say to its valentine?

You give my life porpoise!

What did the owl tell its true love?

Owl be yours forever!

How do you get a squirrel to be your valentine?

Act a little nuts!

What do you call the pigeon god of love?

Coo-pid.

What do you call it when fish fall in love?

Guppy love.

Did you hear the one about the bed bugs who fell in love?

They got married in the spring.

Why do horses make great couples?

They have stable relationships!

What did the pig say to its Valentine's Day date?

I won't go bacon your heart!

What did the bat say to girlfriend on Valentine's Day?

You're sure fun to hang around with.

What did the snake say to her boyfriend on Valentine's Day?

Come here and give me a little hiss.

What did the lizard say to woo his valentine?

There are chameleon reasons why I love you!

Why do bears make for the most honest Valentine's Day dates?

They can't help but bear their souls to each other!

What did the deer say to woo his valentine?

I'm very fawn of you!

What did the tortoise say to his sweetheart?

You're turtle-ly awesome!

What did the tuna say to her boyfriend on Valentine's Day?

I'm o-fish-ally in love with you!

What do you call a sheep covered in chocolate?

A chocolate baa.

How did the spider know she was in love?

Her boyfriend gave her butterflies!

Why did the cats get married on Valentine's Day?

They were Purr-fect for each other.

What did the elephant say to her boyfriend on

Valentine's Day?

I love you a ton.

What did the boy squirrel say to the girl squirrel on

Valentine's Day?

I'm nuts about you!

What did the girl squirrel say back to the boy squirrel?

You're nuts so bad yourself!

What did the bee say to his Valentine's Day sweetheart?

You are bee-utiful! Will you bee mine?

What do porcupines say when they kiss?

Ouch!

Which one of Santa's reindeer can you always spot on Valentine's Day?

Cupid.

What did the rabbit tell his Valentine?

Did you know some-bunny loves you?

Why did the rooster cross the road?

He wanted to impress the chicks.

Chapter 3: Q&A Challenge

"They invented hugs to let people know you love them without saying anything" ~ Bil Keane

What did the light bulb tell the light switch?

You make my day brighter.

Why does Cupid always win at card games?

Because he's a Valentine's Cardshark.

Why is lettuce the most loving of all the vegetables?

Because it's all heart!

Did you hear the one about the angels that got married on Valentine's Day?

They lived harpily ever after!

What do single people say to each other on Valentine's Day?

Happy Independent Day!

What's the best part of Valentine's?

The day after when sweets are on sale!

Did you hear about the man who promised to get his valentine a diamond?

He took her to see a baseball game!

What kind of bear has no teeth?

A Gummy Bear!

A doctor and a bus driver both love the same woman. Before going away on a long trip, the bus driver gave his sweetheart a bag of apples. Why?

Because an apple a day keeps the doctor away!

Why are you and your valentine like a sock?

You make a great pair!

What vegetable makes the best valentine?

A sweet potato!

Why did the old man call his valentine "dentures?"

Because he couldn't smile without her!

How do you show your valentine who's boss?

Hold up a mirror!

Why does a valentine make you feel like a snowflake?

Because you've fallen for them!

What's the perfect crime?

Stealing your Valentine's heart!

What's the best way to fall?

In love!

What did the astronaut's valentine say when he proposed to her in space?

I'm so excited, I can't breathe!

What's better than being madly in love?

Being happily in love!

Who gets the most Valentine's Day cards every year?

The postman!

Why does 1 love 0?

Because she's always around!

What do cavemen and cavewomen do on Valentine's Day?

Go clubbing!

How do you know that a knife thrower really loves his partner?

He always misses her!

Why do people always cry at love stories written in braille?

They're so touching!

When isn't it romantic to steal someone's heart?

During surgery!

What do you call that feeling when you fall for your valentine?

Your common sense leaving.

Why were the girl's feet getting cold?

Because her valentine knocked her socks off!

What's the difference between like and love?

About two letters!

How do lightbulbs celebrate Valentine's Day?

They go out together!

Why isn't space a good place to take your Valentine's Day date?

It doesn't have any atmosphere!

Why is your valentine like a camera?

Because you smile every time you look at them!

How is your valentine like a broom?

They can both sweep you off your feet!

Are you a Pokemon?

Because I want to choose you!

How did the time traveler's relationship end?

It was over before it even began!

Why shouldn't you break somebody's heart?

They only have one!

Why did the artist ask the colour green to be his valentine?

Because he loved it more than blue and yellow combined!

What is it like dating gravity?

It has its ups and downs!

Why is a relationship without trust like a phone without service?

All you do is play games!

What did the hamburger buy his sweetheart on Valentine's Day?

An onion ring.

What happened when the monster kissed his one true love?

He left his lip prints on the mirror!

What does Cupid always order with his pizza?

Wings.

What indoor sport is Cupid the best at?

Darts.

What card game does Cupid always win at?

Hearts.

Why should you never make fun of your valentine's choices?

You're one of them!

Why did the boy ask his asthma to be his valentine?

It took his breath away!

What does a cupcake call their valentine?

Their love muffin.

What did the envelope say to his stamp on Valentine's Day?

I feel like I can go anywhere so long as we stick together.

Who is Cupid's favorite superhero?

Arrow.

What happened to the couple who met in a revolving door?

They're still going around together!

Why do valentines have hearts on them?

Because brains would be really gross!

What was the French cat's favorite dessert to eat on Valentine's Day?

Chocolate mousse.

Chapter 4: Knock-Knock Jokes

"There's a long life ahead of you and it's going to be beautiful, as long as you keep loving and hugging each other" ~ Yoko Ono

Knock, knock

Who's there?

Olive

Olive who?

Olive you!

Knock, knock

Who's there?

Sherwood

Sherwood who?

Sherwood like to be your valentine!

Knock, knock

Who's there?

Pooch

Pooch who?

Pooch your arms around me, baby!

Knock, knock

Who's there?

Jamaica

Jamaica who?

Jamaica valentine for me yet?

Knock, knock

Who's there?

Luke

Luke who?

Luke who got a valentine!

Knock, knock

Who's there?

Mary

Mary who?

Mary me, please!

Knock, knock

Who's there?

Orange.

Orange who?

Orange you glad that it's Valentine's Day already?

Knock, knock

Who's there?

Peas

Peas who?

Peas be my valentine!

Knock, knock

Who's there?

Will

Will who?

Will you be my valentine?

Knock, knock

Who's there?

Yule

Yule who?

Yule never know how much I love you!

Knock, knock

Who's there?

Egg!

Egg who?

Egg-cited to be your valentine!

Knock, knock

Who's there?

Howard

Howard who?

Howard you like a big kiss?

Knock, knock

Who's there?

Abby

Abby who?

Abby Valentine's Day!

Knock, knock

Who's there?

Eyesore

Eyesore who?

Eyesore do like you!

Knock, knock

Who's there?

Al

Al who?

Al be your valentine if you'll be mine!

Knock, knock

Who's there?

Bea

Bea who?

Bea my valentine?

Knock, knock

Who's there?

Honeydew

Honeydew who?

Honeydew you want to be my valentine?

Knock, knock

Who's there?

Emma

Emma who?

Emma hoping I get lots of cards this Valentine's Day!

Knock, knock

Who's there?

Iguana

Iguana who?

Iguana hold your hand.

Knock, knock

Who's there?

Fangs

Fangs who?

Fangs for being my valentine!

Knock, knock

Who's there?

Fonda

Fonda who?

Fonda you!

Knock, knock

Who's there?

Francie

Francie who?

Francie being my valentine?

Knock, knock

Who's there?

Halibut

Halibut who?

Halibut being my valentine?

Knock, knock

Who's there?

Iris

Iris who?

Iris you were here!

Knock, knock

Who's there?

Kisses

Kisses who?

Kisses your lucky Valentine's Day!

Knock, knock

Who's there?

Zoo

Zoo who?

Zoo you want to be my valentine?

Knock, knock

Who's there?

Stopwatch

Stopwatch who?

Stopwatch you are doing and have a happy Valentine's Day!

Knock, knock

Who's there?

Iva

Iva who?

Iva sore hand from knocking!

Knock, knock

Who's there?

Witches

Witches who?

Witches the way to the Valentine's Day dance?

Knock, knock

Who's there?

Al

Al who?

Al give you a kiss if you open this door!

Knock, knock

Who's there?

Amish

Amish who?

Aw, how sweet. I miss you too!

Knock, knock

Who's there?

Fiddle

Fiddle who?

Fiddle make me happy if you would be my valentine!

Knock, knock

Who's there?

I love you!

I love you who?

Don't ask who, because it's you!

Knock, knock

Who's there?

Aldo

Aldo who?

Aldo anything for my valentine!

Knock, knock

Who's there?

Owl

Owl who?

Owl be happy to be your valentine!

Knock, knock

Who's there?

Juno

Juno who?

Juno I love you, right?

Knock, knock

Who's there?

Candice

Candice who?

Candice be love I'm feeling now?

Knock, knock

Who's there?

Needle

Needle who?

Needle a date for this Valentine's Day?

Knock, knock

Who's there?

Pauline

Pauline who?

I think I'm Pauline in love with you!

Knock, knock

Who's there?

Cheese

Cheese who?

Cheese a nice girl for being my valentine!

Knock, knock

Who's there?

Mower

Mower who?

I like you mower and mower every day!

Knock knock

Who's there?

A door

A door who?

I a door you!

Chapter 5: Situations

"Love yourself first and everything else falls into line. You really have to love yourself to get anything done in this world."~ **Lucille Ball**

A woman woke up on Valentine's Day morning and told her husband, "I had a dream that you gave me the most gorgeous and expensive diamond necklace I had ever seen as a Valentine's Day present. What do you think it means?" "You'll know tonight," her husband told her before he left for work. That night, the husband came back with a gift-wrapped present for her.

Absolutely thrilled, the woman opened it up to find a book titled "The Meaning of Dreams."

A few days before Valentine's, a young student studied really hard to pass a maths test but the teacher was known for being a tough marker. When the student got his test back on Valentine's Day, he saw that he had a B-minus. Hoping to change the teacher's mind, the student sent their maths teacher an expensive box of chocolates in the shape of a heart with an inscription that read "Be mine."

The following day, the teacher sent the student a late Valentine's Day card.

It read, "Thanks for the chocolates, but your grade is still be mine-us."

Noticing that it was Valentine's Day next week, a boyfriend decided to see what his girlfriend desired. "What type of gift do you want this Valentine's Day?" he asked her.

"Well, I don't know," she replied coyly.

"Okay then," her boyfriend said. "I'll give you another year to think about it."

Matt wanted to get his girlfriend an expensive bracelet for Valentine's Day as a surprise so he went to the finest jewellery store in his city. After picking out a beautiful piece, the jeweller asked if he wanted to get his girlfriend's name engraved on it. After thinking about it for a minute, Matt decided to get it engraved to "His one and only."

"That's very romantic," the jeweller told him.

"Not really," Matt said, "This way if we break up, I can use it again."

On Valentine's Day, a young boy was walking through the forest that was filled with mushrooms when suddenly a talking fox came up to him. "Be careful where you step," the fox told him, "if you step on an orange mushroom then you will end up with the valentine of the ugliest person in the whole wide world."

The boy carefully watched his step, avoiding any and all of the orange mushrooms.

Suddenly, a beautiful girl appeared and approached him.

"I guess you're my valentine now," she told him.

"Why?" the boy asked.

"I just stepped on one of those awful orange mushrooms," she replied.

Two aerials met on a roof one Valentine's Day. They fell in love immediately and got married.

Their wedding ceremony wasn't very fancy but the reception was excellent.

A beautiful girl spent all of Valentine's Day waiting to see what her boyfriend was going to get her. After school, she went over to his house for dinner. Instead of roses and chocolates, he surprised her with a plate of cannoli.

"What is this for?" she asked him.

"I cannoli be happy when I'm with you," he said with a wink.

Becky and Sarah were drawing pictures in the living of Becky's house. Sarah drew a picture of a knight rescuing a princess from a dragon and Becky drew a picture of herself and her neighbour, Ryan. "Who's that?" Sarah asked.

"The boy next door," Becky answered. "Someday I'm going to marry him, you know."

"Why? Is he cute?" Sarah asked.

"No," Becky sighed. "But mum won't let me cross the street."

A plate decided to take out a fork for an expensive Valentine's Day supper. When the waiter came to take their order he asked if the plate and fork wanted it on one bill or two.

The plate looked at the fork and replied, "Don't worry, love, dinner's on me."

Sally was five years old. She loved sweets even more than her mother did. On Valentine's Day, Sally's father brought home a big box of heart-shaped chocolates for Sally's mum. The next day, the box of chocolates still had a lot of them left. Sally opened the box, reached in and touched one of the sweets.

"Now, now, Sally," her mother said, "you will have to eat it now that you touched it."

Thinking for a minute, Sally reached into the box and swept her hand over the top of all the chocolates. "Well, now I guess I have to eat them all," she said with a smile.

A young boy asked his crush if she would be his Valentine. She told him she would but then the entire time that they were together on the playground, the young boy pretended that he was a Transformer. This annoyed his valentine like crazy. "If you don't stop that," she told him as she turned her back and walked away, "then I'm leaving.

"Wait," the young boy said with an outstretched arm, "I can change!"

David wanted to ask Jessica to be his Valentine but he was too shy to just come right out and ask her directly. Instead, David approached Jessica at the end of class and asked her if she liked him.

"Well," she said, "as far as boys go, I guess that you're alright."

Smiling from ear to ear, David was about to ask her if she would go to the Valentine's Day dance with him when she continued.

"But the further you go, the better!"

A scary boy monster called up his girl-monster on Valentine's day to ask if she had received the big red heart he had sent her. "Yes, I did. You're so thoughtful," she said. "Thank you."

"Well," the boy monster said, "is it still beating?"

A couple was out to dinner for Valentine's Day when suddenly the girl looked over at her boyfriend and asked him, "Do you love me?"

"Of course I love you," he replied while looking at the restaurant's menu.

"Then whisper something soft and sweet in my ear," the girl told him.

Without taking his eyes off the menu, the boy leaned in close to the girl's ear and gently whispered, "Lemon meringue pie."

A handsome young Prince decided that it was time for him to be married. However, he couldn't just wed any Princess. The Prince would only get married to the most beautiful Princess in all the lands. He heard rumors of a great beauty on the other side of the world and so he set off on a grand adventure to find her.

After battling dragons and trolls and overcoming all kinds of obstacles, the Prince, at last, made his way to the Princess's castle and asked the Guards to see the King. Dressed in the finest clothing he could afford, the Prince confidently strolled up to the King and told him, "I have come from the other side of the world, having heard rumours of your daughter's beauty. I have battled monsters and beasts, braved storms and seas, all so that I may ask for your daughter's hand in marriage."

The king scoffed, "Well, you'll have to take the rest of her too or there'll be no deal!"

Did you enjoy the book?

If you did, we are ecstatic. If not, please write your complaint to us and we will make sure to fix it.

If you're feeling generous, there is something important that you can help me with – tell other people that you enjoyed the book.

Ask a grown up to write about it on Amazon. When they do, more people will find out about the book. It also lets Amazon know that we are making kids around the world laugh. Even a few words and ratings would go a long way.

If you have any ideas or jokes that you think are super funny, please let us know. We would love to hear from you. Our email address is - riddleland@riddlelandforkids.com

Alert: Try Not to Laugh Challenge Bonus Jokes

Join our special Facebook Joke Group at
~Riddleland For Kids~

or

send an email to:

Riddleland@riddlelandforkids.com

and you will get the following

- 50 Bonus Jokes and Riddles
- An Entry in Our Monthly Giveaway of $50 Amazon Gift card!
- Early Access to new books

We draw a new winner each month and will contact you via email or the facebook group.
Good Luck!

Would you like your jokes and riddles to be featured in our next book?

We are having **a contest** to see who are the smartest or funniest boys and girls in the world!

1) **Creative and Challenging Riddles**
2) **Tickle Your Funny Bone Contest**

Parents, please email us your child's "Original" Riddle or Joke **and he or she could win a $50 Amazon gift card and be featured in our next book.**

Here are the rules:

1) It must be challenging for the riddles and funny for the jokes!

2) It must be 100% Original and not something from the Internet! It is easy to find out!

3) You can submit both a joke and a riddle as they are 2 separate contests.

4) No help from the parents unless they are as funny as you.

5) Winners will be announced via email or our facebook group – Riddleland for kids

6) Please also mention what book you purchased.

7) Email us at Riddleland@riddlelandforkids.com

Other Fun Children's Books for Kids!
Riddles Series

Encourage your kids to think outside of the box with these Fun and Creative Riddles!

Get them on Amazon

Try Not to Laugh Challenge Series

Would You Rather... Series

Get them on Amazon
or our website at www.riddlelandforkids.com

About the Riddleland

Riddleland is a mum + dad run publishing company. We are passionate about creating fun and innovative books to help children develop their reading skill and fall in love with reading. If you have suggestions for us or want to work with us, shoot us an email at riddleland@riddlelandforkids.com

Our family's favorite quote

"Creativity is an area in which younger people have a tremendous advantage since they have an endearing habit of always questioning past wisdom and authority." – Bill Hewlett